W9-CQR-119

Portrait of
OREGON

Portrait of America Series

Portrait of
OREGON

Photography by Ray Atkeson
Text by Tom Barr

 GRAPHIC ARTS CENTER PUBLISHING COMPANY
Portland, Oregon

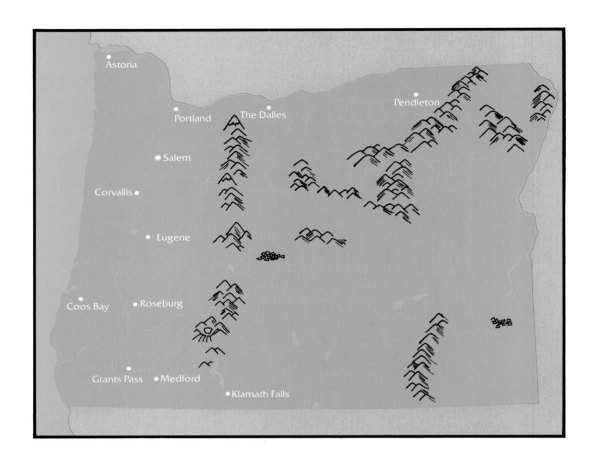

Cover: *Oneonta Creek cascades over lava as it twists down a narrow gorge to the Columbia River.*

Title Page: *The sun sets over the Pacific Ocean silhouetting Haystack Rock and The Needles at Cannon Beach.*

International Standard Book Number 0-912856-52-1
Library of Congress Catalog Number 79-91507
Copyright © MCMLXXX by Graphic Arts Center Publishing Company
P.O. Box 10306 • Portland, Oregon 97210 • 503/226-2402
Typesetting • Paul O. Giesey/Adcrafters
Printing • Moore Lithograph, Inc.
Binding • Lincoln & Allen
Printed in the United States of America
Sixth Printing

Contents

The Coast

"What can we do with the western coast," thundered Daniel Webster, "...rockbound, cheerless, uninviting and not a harbor on it. What use have we for such a country?"

Despite opposition from Webster and others, the United States created the Oregon Territory in 1848. By the time Congress admitted it to the union on February 14, 1859 — thus earning it the nickname of "Valentine State" — explorers had been sailing to its shores for over three hundred years. The rugged coast, with its turbulent storms, spouting horns, and rocky headlands, had challenged their courage and seamanship, and often sent them away in defeat.

Sir Francis Drake may have been the first white man to see Oregon's beaches. Fresh from plundering Spanish galleons and fearful of retaliation, he sailed north in 1579 while seeking the Northwest Passage and a safe route home. Drake reached Cape Blanco — the westernmost point of land in Oregon. Claiming Oregon for England, Drake may have landed south of Coos Bay before cold weather and violent storms drove him back to California.

In 1778, the intrepid Englishman, Captain James Cook, came searching for the Northwest Passage. The foremost explorer of his time — a man who had safely landed in Australia, New Zealand and Hawaii and who would later reach British Columbia — Cook was turned away by the Oregon Coast. Sleet and snow storms were so severe that he was unable to land. Fog masked the mouth of the Columbia River, and he missed it as well. Before continuing north to Alaska and the Bering Sea, he named Cape Foulweather, Cape Perpetua, and Cape Arago.

If Captains Drake and Cook had come ashore, they would have discovered sheer cliffs rising abruptly from white, sandy beaches to mountains green with forests. They would have heard the sound of wheeling gulls piercing the roar of crashing breakers. Today the Pacific still roars against Oregon's craggy cliffs and rocky caverns carved by wind and pounding waves. There are still jagged reefs, jutting headlands, and offshore monoliths abandoned by the coastline to be sculptured and consumed by the tides. And life in the sea is still plentiful; salmon, tuna, halibut, and shellfish — clams, oysters and the succulent Dungeness crab abound. The storms of winter still rage, but now they are enjoyed from the shore as one of nature's most spectacular performances. The rugged Oregon Coast, which thwarted exploration, brought disaster and even death to earlier investigators, has become a favorite recreation area of the twentieth century.

The shoreline, which marks the eternal battle between land and sea, has given in to human habitation. Now villages, towns, and small cities crowd close to the ocean and nestle in secluded coves. A modern highway — U.S. 101 strings them together along the 400-mile coastline. Giving the lie to Daniel Webster's pessimism, 23 established port districts handle over 4,000 vessels annually.

The public owns Oregon's beaches. Of the 233 parks maintained by the State Parks and Recreation branch of the Oregon Department of Transportation, (totaling over 92,000 acres throughout the state) 36 parks, waysides, and recreation areas dot the coastline adjacent to the highway. There are also over 70 free boat ramps and some areas where you can drive a car onto the beach.

Each year, vacationers come by the thousands to skin-dive and surf, hunt for agates and seashells, or build driftwood fires in the twilight. Others are attracted to the superb fishing or simply to discover the gentle, delicate harmony of ecological communities in the tide pools. Along these four hundred miles of promontories, estuaries, and inlets are innumerable places to enchant the mind and delight the eye.

The first exploration took place on the northern beach where nature was most lavish with her handiwork — the shoreline edging the Columbia River's entry into the Pacific. Today the greatest concentration of population is found here. Astoria, the fur-trading center established by John Jacob Astor on the river's south bank in 1811, survives as a lumber port and commercial fishing center. Fort Stevens has stood west of Astoria since 1862. In 1942, when a Japanese submarine lobbed a barrage into the fort, it became the only military installation in the continental United States to be fired upon by a foreign power since the War of 1812. Fort Clatsop — south of the river mouth — has been reconstructed on the original site occupied by Lewis and Clark during the winter of 1805-1806.

The rugged Clatsop beaches extending south to Tillamoook Head host the heart of the razor clam population in Oregon. On weekends with minus tides, diggers cluster on these beaches and on the 40,000 acres of bay-clam producing areas on eleven

Left: Boiler Bay, south of Lincoln City was named after a ship wrecked here in 1910, lodging its boiler, which is still visible, among the rocks at the upper right.

major inlets of the Oregon Coast. On their way home, many of these sportsmen travel through Tillamook County, nationally acclaimed for its cheeses and other dairy products. The forests of the Coast Range east of Tillamook still bear the scars of three disastrous fires. In 1933 an inferno which lasted 12 days consumed 375 square miles of timber land. History repeated itself with a 17 day fire in 1939 which burned 300 square miles and another which lasted 53 days in 1945. The last fire claimed 280 square miles of timber.

Travelers have come to Newport since 1866 to fish in Yaquina Bay, search for agates, or journey north to the rip tides and spouting horns at Depoe Bay. In this region, one may also venture out in the stillness that follows a storm and find prized fishing floats made in Japan, Germany, or Russia. Each year visitors pick up hundreds of these colored, glass balls. Some have floated over 4,000 miles to rest on Oregon beaches.

While Newport is one of the oldest resorts on the coast, Indians used the Yachats area, 20 miles to the south, as a fishing grounds centuries before Europeans discovered America. Tribes came from up and down the coast to harvest mussels and smelt. The shells were thrown into mounds, some of which date back 500 to 1,000 years. Today, Yachats is still one of the few places in the world where smelt come to shore to spawn.

Farther down the coast, Sea Lion Caves have been compared both in size and coloring to the Mediterranean's famed Blue Grotto of Capri. They are the only natural mainland sea lion home in the world. Inside this 1,500-foot long cavern — accessible to tourists by elevator — 2,000-pound bulls watch over their harems as small pups cavort against a background of blending greens, pinks, reds, and purples. Outside, the skies and rocks are frequently filled with birds, for the caves are also a haven for gulls, cormorants, pigeon guillemots, and tufted puffins, or sea parrots.

The Oregon Dunes National Recreation Area stretches for 61 miles along the Oregon Coast from Florence to Coos Bay. Extending three miles inland, the dunes are dotted with a chain of small lakes and ponds and a scattering of half-buried pines and sitka spruce. The dunes offer a special excitement unlike any other place on the coast. Both dune buggy enthusiasts and nature lovers delight in the way the dunes change size and shape with the whims of the wind. Flat rolling mounds can shift to become 300-foot high sand mountains within hours.

Rhododendrons burn brightly on the landscape at Coos Bay, where fishermen cast their lines into the surf along the stony promontories. Although two ecological zones overlap near Coos Bay and provide a greater variety of sea life than virtually anywhere else along the Pacific coast, the city's economy is based not on fish and flowers, but on timber. All but two of Oregon's 36 counties manufacture lumber and wood products — much of it for export to other nations. More lumber is shipped out of Coos Bay than any other port in the United States.

Spring comes to the southern corner of the Oregon Coast in a blaze of brilliant wildflowers vying for attention with the sculptured capes, bays, and blues of the Pacific Ocean. Pink and white morning glories, violets, primroses, and scotch broom brighten fields and roadsides. Along with the wild blossoms, comes a profusion of domesticated flowers. Ninety percent of America's Easter lilies are raised in Brookings, the southernmost city on the coast, and Bandon, which is also famous for its cheese and cranberries. Brookings, raises daffodils as well as lillies and is the site of Azalea State Park, which has 25 acres of azaleas, some 15 to 20 feet high and over 400 years old.

For many, a trip to the Oregon beach is an annual ritual — a rite to welcome or celebrate summer, or to mark the passing of autumn and the coming of another winter. Like the seasons the coast is eternal, yet constantly changing, endlessly fascinating.

This Haystack Rock—the larger of the two so called on the Oregon coast—is located offshore near Pacific City, a town famous for dory fishing.

*Horse-drawn vehicles and early automobiles used to
cross this rock ledge at Hug Point, south of Cannon Beach,
to get to the flat beaches beyond.*

The broad sandy beaches of Neahkahnie and
Manzanita stretch southward to Nehalem Bay in
Tillamook County.

Overleaf: Cape Kiwanda and a lone seastack
withstand the storm-whipped waves that churn
against them.

11

*As viewed from the forested slopes near Cape Meares
south of Tillamook Bay, offshore rocks testify to
Oregon's rugged coastline.*

The Oregon Dunes National Recreation Area, a shifting sea of sand up to five miles wide, covers 61 miles of central coastline between Florence and Coos Bay.

Prevailing summer winds etch ripples in the dunes,
yet subsurface moisture permits grasses and trees to
grow throughout the region.

Huge pinnacles and flat-topped rocks stand offshore from Bandon Beach just west of the town of Bandon, founded by the Irishman Lord Bennett.

*Autumn fog filters the morning sunlight in one of
the numerous parks and recreation areas along the
400-mile coast.*

The sun sets between twin seastacks called The Needles, a favorite tourist spot at Cannon Beach on the north coast.

*South of Cannon Beach, capes and heads dominate
the coast. Here Neahkahnie Mountain is seen from
Cape Falcon.*

Seagulls stand resting along the beach —a primeval
zone of compromise and conflict where change is the
only constant.

The beach at Devil's Elbow State Park is speckled with seagulls while, above, the Heceta Head Lighthouse warns ships of the reefs during darkness and fog.

The 1,500-acre Samuel H. Boardman State Park contains rugged southern headlands and a plaque honoring this man as the "Father of Oregon State Parks."

The Cascades

The mile-high wall of the Cascade Mountains cuts across the length of Oregon from the Columbia River to the California border. The 260 by 50 mile area of this magnificent range is an invaluable repository of natural resources and an alpine playground for all seasons. It is a tableland of mountainside meadows, white-water streams, and hundreds of tranquil lakes surrounded by evergreen forests and walls of stones. Atop this beautiful barricade are the "fire mountains" of Indian legends, majestic volcanos capped with snow and streaked with glaciers.

The Cascades separate eastern and western Oregon, and give each region a distinctive image, character, and climate. As a weather barrier, they determine vegetation, agricultural production, and ultimately the economy of the two regions.

Pacific breezes warmed by the Japanese currents and laden with moisture, drop 40 to 85 inches of rain annually on western Oregon. Because of the abundant precipitation and temperatures that seldom rise above 100 degrees (F) or drop below zero, the western one-third of the state is the Oregon of travel posters and popular image: rolling meadowlands of sweet green grass and evergreen forests of timber 200-300 feet tall.

When the wet winds and clouds reach the Cascades—over 100 miles inland from the ocean—the moisture condenses, and much of it falls as rain, sleet, and snow. East of the crest, precipitation drops dramatically to eight or ten inches per year. Temperatures soar as high as 119 degrees in summer and plummet to record-setting −54 degrees in winter. Forests change from the towering Douglas firs, ferns, and tangled underbrush of the west to open woodlands of Ponderosa pine and juniper. The eastern low country is speckled with sagebrush, stone mesas, and treeless lava flows broken by patches of flatland desert.

If the mountains are a barrier, they are also a great benefactor. In the Cascade high country, snowfalls reach depths of 40 to 50 feet per season. Out of these snowpacks and glaciers flow Oregon's three major rivers — the Rogue, the Umpqua, and the Willamette. They are also the source of the McKenzie, Calapooya, Santiam, Metolius, Mollalla, and Clackamas, as well as countless creeks, streams, and rivulets. The life-giving rivers, in turn, provide irrigation and drinking water, energy, fish, transportation, and a variety of recreational activities.

It has been said that Oregon has enough timber to build a floor across Massachusetts twice over, rebuild every house in the United States, and still have lumber to spare. It is the nation's largest producer of lumber and wood products. Over one-third of Oregon is timberland, and of the state's 13 national forests, seven are in the Cascades. The Willamette National Forest alone accounts for 10 percent of all lumber cut in national forests. The western slopes yield Douglas fir for lumber, plywood, and wood pulp, and western hemlock for boxes, ladders, furniture, sashes, and doors. Ponderosa pine from the eastern slopes and southern Oregon becomes moldings, shelving, caskets, and boats. Oregon produces 50 percent of the nation's plywood, 25 percent of its hardwood, and 20 percent of its shingles. The yield is kept in balance with growth — that is, the amounts harvested each year are equal to, but do not exceed, the number of trees planted through natural and planned reforestation.

In ages past the Cascades were formed of volcanic rock that was then ground down and reshaped through centuries of glacial action. While the complete range begins in southern British Columbia and extends to northern California, the Oregon section has the highest plateau and some of the most spectacular peaks, their symmetrical pinnacles spaced like silvery sentry towers atop a green and gray fortress.

The Cascades were the subject of many Indian legends. Three of the "fire mountains" were created, the Indians said, when the Supreme Being became angry at his two sons for quarreling over a beautiful maiden. In his rage, he destroyed the "Bridge of the Gods" — a great stone arch that in legend spanned the Columbia River at Cascade Locks. The debris from the bridge became the Cascades, and the two sons became Mount Hood and Washington's Mount Adams, only to continue their quarrel by throwing boulders and sheets of fire at each other. The third principal in the triangle — the beautiful maiden — lives on as Washington's Mount Saint Helens.

At 11,235 feet, Mount Hood is the monarch of the Oregon mountains and the highest point in the state. During the November-to-May sports season, 260,000 snow enthusiasts come to enjoy Mount Hood's six major ski areas and other recreation facilities. Over four million people per year hike

Left: Ramona Falls breaks into silvery veils as it cascades down a cliff of lava basalt in Mount Hood National Forest.

through its 1,169,840-acre national forest. Mount Hood, second only to Japan's Mount Fujiyama as the most climbed snow-capped peak in the world, is one of the few areas in the Northwest that offers summer ice climbing. Other visitors fish and photograph the deep blue mountain lakes, ride snow cats to the 10,000-foot level, hike wilderness trails to a dozen glaciers, or backpack around the mountain and through the forest.

Mount Hood, which erupted as recently as 1865, is one of the few remaining dormant volcanos in the United States. Called "Wy'East" by the Indians, it was renamed by Lieutenant William Broughten of the British Royal Navy to honor Rear Admiral Samuel Hood. (Broughten had sailed up the Columbia to the Sandy River in 1792 and claimed the Oregon country for England.) During the migrations to the Willamette Valley in the 1840s, Mount Hood stood as a landmark and one of the last obstacles to be surmounted on the Oregon Trail.

Five peaks frame the horizon of central Oregon. Pioneers called The Three Sisters, Faith, Hope and Charity. Sometimes they needed all three to get over the Cascades. One pioneer wrote: "Some men's heart's died within them...women sat by the roadside and cried...we went down mountains so steep that we had to let our wagons down with ropes... My wife and I...carried the loading of our wagons upon our backs by piecemeal, as our cattle were hardly able to haul up our empty wagon."

Dominating the entire Deschutes area, the Three Sisters have intrigued geologists for decades. Before the Ice Age glaciers eroded away much of its bulk, North Sister may have been one-fourth again as large as it is today. At 10,085 feet, it is the oldest of the three. Middle Sister, 10,047 feet, is second in age, and South Sister, 10,358 feet, is the youngest of Oregon's Cascade peaks.

The other two peaks in this area are Bachelor Butte, 9,060 feet high, and Broken Top, 9,152 feet. On Bachelor the skiing season usually begins before Thanksgiving and lasts through Memorial Day. During the summer the United States Ski Team uses its perpetual snow fields as a training ground. Broken Top with its seemingly razor-sharp ridges, cliffs, and steep slopes, is one of the most rugged mountains in the Cascade Range. Waters from its glaciers provide the major portion of the drinking water for the city of Bend.

Mount Jefferson, 10,495 feet, 43 miles south of Mount Hood, and Three Fingered Jack, 7,841 feet, stand ready to challenge advanced mountain climbers, as does Mount Washington, 7,802 feet, with its rugged lava beds, craters, chimneys, and sheer rock. With over 100 lakes in the Mount Jefferson Wilderness Area alone, these mountains also provide sport for fishermen.

Although man has learned to use and enjoy the Cascades, he has fortunately never been able to manipulate them or disturb their majesty. Nature reigns here, for the most part a benevolent tyrant.

The ice-cold waters of the Metolius River descend from high on the eastern flank of the Cascades near Mount Jefferson.

Overleaf: Cloud caps band over the craggy crest of Mount Jefferson, Oregon's second highest peak at 10,495 feet.

Mixed conifers and an understory of vine maple and ferns are typical of the Cascade forests at lower elevations.

Mount Hood's glacier and snow-laden volcanic cone
towers to 11,235 feet—a counterpoint to the Hood
River Valley on a warm summer day.

Deep winter snows accumulate on the rim of
Crater Lake National Park where seepage and snow
melt keep the level of the lake amazingly close to
a constant.

Past the rugged shoulder of Larch Mountain, lenticular clouds momentarily ring Mount Hood, whose height and mass often create local weather phenomena.

Lava flows (which mushroomed up from fissures at the base of South Sister) terminate at Devils Lake—evidence of relatively recent volcanic activity.

The North Santiam River on its way to the Willamette, rushes through a rocky gorge at Niagara Park in the western foothills of the Cascades.

*Back from the sea, a salmon leaps upstream as
it returns to spawn in the place where it was born.*

Goodpasture Bridge, spanning the McKenzie River near Leaburg, was built in 1938, and is typical of the surviving covered bridges of the 1920s and 1930s over Cascade streams.

Lower Proxy Falls is located near the McKenzie Pass
Highway in the Three Sisters Wilderness Area, a section
of streams, lakes, and mountains between
Eugene and Bend.

Autumn color highlights Eagle Creek Punch Bowl, a
famous lava pool in Mount Hood National Forest.

Sparks Lake nestles below Broken Top Mountain (9,152 feet) along the Cascade Lakes Highway in Deschutes National Forest.

The Cascades is a rolling forested range, punctuated
by such snow-capped volcanoes as Mount Bachelor
in the foreground and the Three Sisters beyond.

On the north wall of Mount Hood, Coe and Ladd
Glaciers slowly carve and shape the mountain under
their weight.

Wahkeena Falls tumbles in and out of the midday sun in its deep moss- and fern-lined gorge in Mount Hood National Forest.

The Columbia River and Willamette Valley

The Columbia River and the Willamette Valley have been participants in a parade of history since at least the end of the last Ice Age. Acting as a drain for the huge inland lakes formed by melting glaciers, the Columbia swelled to fifty times its present volume. Along with the deluges, came giant boulders and icebergs as large as buildings, which scoured and sculptured the basalts of the Columbia River Gorge, creating crevasses, canyons and ravines, and eroding away soft soils to expose sheer cliffs of solid rock. At the end of the Ice Age, the Columbia covered the future sites of Portland and the northern Willamette Valley with from 125 to 325 feet of water.

Through the ensuing millennia the Columbia grew into the giant river that it is today, beginning in Columbia Lake in the Canadian Rockies and flowing for 1,270 miles to the Pacific Ocean. Until the American Captain Robert Gray discovered and named it for his merchant ship in 1792, the Columbia had been known only in legends as the Oregon, or "Great River of the West." During the early 1800s the river and its gorge were the main avenue of Northwest exploration and trade. Indian canoes knew it well; Lewis and Clark braved its treacherous rapids on their way to the Pacific Ocean, and scows, paddlewheelers, steamboats, and light navy ships followed as history unfolded. With the establishment of the Washington Territory in 1853, the last 300 miles of the Columbia became the Oregon-Washington border.

Today eleven hydroelectric dams breach the Columbia. Bonneville and The Dalles are in the gorge, and to the east, upriver, lie John Day and McNary. Now the Columbia is the second largest navigable river in the United States; only the Mississippi exceeds it. It irrigates more land west of the Continental Divide than any other stream, and together with eleven major tributaries, drains 259,000 square miles in seven states and Canada. It is the West's primary salmon-producing stream and it is a major source of waterpower. As an energy resource, it is far mightier than the Mississippi, which has a larger watershed.

When you travel through the 60-mile length of the Columbia River Gorge, mesmerized by the tranquillity of nature and the smooth flow of water, you can forget the river's turbulent past. Technology has tamed the Columbia — harnessed its power and reduced it in many places to a series of languid lakes. Celilo Falls, where the river used to rage in torrents of milk-white water, now lie beneath a placid lake formed by The Dalles Dam. The lake is often crowded with pleasure boats, swimmers and water-skiers. Its shores and banks — once the "great mart of the west" where Indian tribes came from afar to fish and trade horses, buffalo robes, beads, axes, knives, and cloth — comprise a park with picnic and playground facilities.

Human industry and ingenuity have made the magnificent scenery of the canyon available to the visitor. Interstate 80 winds through the 60-mile gorge close to the river, while a "scenic highway" built in 1915 takes travelers into the high ground, close to waterfalls, through ravines, around cliffs and mountainsides, into tunnels cut through rocky promontories. In one stretch, there are eleven waterfalls in eleven miles and a series of switchbacks revealing one spectacular secluded glen or ravine after another. There are hundreds of hiking trails for those who wish to touch the earth and smell spring wildflowers or to backpack along clear streams and less trodden paths.

A closer view shows the gorge is a paradox of ageless landmarks and twentieth-century endeavor. You can find ancient petroglyphs or rock drawings on canyon walls, and petrified trees buried in lava flows. The Hood River Valley is filled with man's fruit orchards, while the slopes above are covered with Douglas fir of the Mount Hood National Forest. You can see islands with sandy beaches and 800-foot slate-gray monoliths that have served as landmarks since the coming of man. Not far away the State Fish Hatchery at Bonneville produces fish by the millions each year. On placid log ponds lumbermen use "bronco" boats to move fallen timber into giant rafts, much as cowboys use horses to direct strays into a herd of cattle. Towboats and barges transport 4.5 million tons of commodities up and down the river and through the gorge every year. Gasoline, fuel oils, and fertilizers go upstream — wheat, barley, rye, and other cargoes return.

Willamette meant "green waters" to the Indians of

Left: Ice and snow-trimmed Multnomah Falls, the state's highest waterfall, plunges 620 feet into the Columbia River Gorge.

the Pacific Northwest. The river, which begins where a muddy stream from the Coast Range merges with white waters from the Cascades, meanders northward for 225 miles through a 125-mile valley to empty into the Columbia at Portland. The Willamette Valley has been the heartland of Oregon since the first French-Canadian employees of the Hudson's Bay Company settled south of the present Oregon City in the 1830s. When the great migration came over the Oregon Trail in the 1840s and 50s, the newcomers headed for the rich Willamette.

Oregon's first settlers were not fortune hunters and gold seekers such as the settlers of many western states, but families and farmers who sought rich, productive farmland. Farming flourished from the beginning and agriculture is still Oregon's second largest income producer. Out of this valley and other parts of Oregon come 50 to 90 percent of the nation's loganberries and fresh market broccoli; 25 to 50 percent of the peppermint, sweet cherries, boysenberries, raspberries, and blackberries; 90 percent of the filberts; and 10 to 25 percent of the hops, peas, and strawberries. In all, Oregon's horn of plenty markets over 100 agricultural products each year.

Over half of the state's population lives within ten miles of the Willamette River, and 60 percent reside within the valley itself. Here lie Oregon's major cities and industries, and its oldest and largest institutions of higher education. The Willamette River flows through Portland, the largest city in the state and the leading dry cargo port on the West Coast; Salem, Oregon's capital and an important food-processing center; and Eugene, whose economy is divided among agriculture, lumber and education.

The Willamette Valley is within easy range of virtually every kind of climate and terrain anyone could want. Most of the major cities are but an hour's drive from the Cascade and Coast Range high country and the Pacific Ocean, and within a day's drive of ancient fossil beds, deserts, and beachfront sand dunes. For those who do not wish to travel far, there is plenty to see and explore in the valley itself.

There are big and small streams for fishing, swimming, canoeing and powerboating. Within its boundaries are state parks, timberlands bordered by snow-crested mountain peaks, and three wildlife refuges, which protect 52 animal and 193 bird species.

Oregon is a state that pays homage to everything from azaleas to rooster crowing. Springfield hosts the annual McKenzie River White Water Parade and the Oregon Broiler Festival and Timberama. Corvallis is the home of Oregon State University and the annual Corvallis International Regatta — one of the largest races of its kind in the nation. Albany boasts the World Championship Timber Carnival and an economy revolving in part around processing titanium and zirconium.

Historic sites include Champoeg Memorial State Park where the first meetings were held to form a territorial government on May 2, 1843, and the Bohemia Mining District which yielded over a million dollars in gold between 1900 and 1910. Champoeg is situated between Salem and Oregon City, and the mining district is located near Cottage Grove. Petrified wood has been found in the western Cascade foothills, and marine fossils have been excavated in Kings Valley. Sweet Home is a rockhound's delight with bonded agates, jasper, crystal-lined geodes, and other semiprecious stones.

Salem has the state's oldest winery as well as Silver Bow State Park where hikers can walk in front of, over, or behind ten waterfalls in two and one-half miles. If all else fails to excite the imagination, there are 157 parks in Lane County alone, and over 120 covered bridges to capture on film.

Too often works of nature are damaged by technological and industrial developments. In the Columbia River, its gorge, and the Willamette Valley, man has used the rivers and the land, and reaped the fruits of his labors without destroying most of the beautiful surroundings.

Silver Creek Falls in the hills east of Salem is framed by the autumn colors of red vine maples and bigleaf maples.

Sunflowers bloom in profusion on the oak-studded slopes near Mosier along the Columbia River.

Sail and power boats crisscross the Columbia River near Portland on a summer weekend, while Mount Hood fills the horizon.

The aurora borealis rose reaches perfection in
Portland's International Rose Test Garden, overlooking
the downtown area in this "City of Roses."

Early morning fog and a mantle of native maple leaves embellish this forest scene on a hill not far from Portland.

The strong, prevailing westerlies that whip through the gorge shape these dunes along the Columbia River in north central Oregon.

*Freighters moored at Astoria cross the same treacher-
ous bar Robert Gray traversed in 1792, when
he discovered and named the Columbia River after
his ship.*

The Willamette River meanders northward for 225
miles through fertile farmland and past this spot at
Champoeg Historical Park before passing through
Portland and flowing into the Columbia.

The state capitol in Salem is topped with a 24-foot statue of an axe-wielding pioneer, symbolic of the settlers who followed the Oregon Trail to the fertile Willamette Valley.

Overleaf: Sunset alpenglow on Mt. Hood punctuates the skyline of Portland, the state's largest metropolitan area, which holds more than one million people and yet retains wilderness on its doorstep.

The mighty Columbia follows a course through
the Cascade Mountains it cut long ago, as it journeys
1,200 miles draining parts of seven states and the
Canadian Rockies.

*Indian paint brush adds a splash of color to the mossy
cliffs of the Oregon side of the gorge.*

Southwestern Oregon

Southwestern Oregon is blessed with an arrangement of mountains and river valleys that has given it a history and character all its own. While the north-south coastal and Cascade formations continue into this region, the Willamette Valley and the Coast Range beyond are replaced here by the Rogue River and the Siskiyous, a jumble of rugged peaks, and sprawling valleys, pellmell streams and quiet lakes. This is Indian war and gold rush country, and a region of "lasts" and "onlys" where the wonders of nature often appear out of context.

Palm trees grow in Langlois on the coast, and for centuries pelicans have been spending the summer at Klamath Falls, 140 miles inland. The kalmiopsis, a small shrub resembling a rhododendron, is the oldest member of the heath family, predating the Ice Age, and the only plant in its genus. It grows along the banks of the Umpqua River and on the slopes of the Siskiyou National Forest and nowhere else. These ancient slopes and peaks are also a haven for the several species of orchids, gentians, darlingtonia, and numerous odd members of the lily family. Near Riddle, green nickel ore is found in abundance; this small community has the only nickel mine in the United States.

This part of the state has a diversified economy. Rugged and beautiful scenery, unusual natural formations, and inviting lakes and rivers all contribute to a healthy tourist trade. Sportsman flock to the Klamath Lakes region, famed for its duck and geese hunting, and the Rogue River, renowned for its salmon and steelhead runs.

The lumber business is evident to eye and ear in mountains stacked from base to summit with tall fir trees. From Roseburg, Interstate 5, the state's main southbound artery, swirls around up and down for 75 miles until it reaches Grants Pass, where it opens onto the Rogue River Valley and the hazy vistas of the Siskiyou Mountains. Around these mountain curves, huge Kenworth and Mack trucks rumble out of the forest on their way to the mills. Nothing is wasted anymore — edgings covered with bark are diverted into stick mills and come out broom and shovel handles; bark and sawdust are hauled away to be mixed with glue, baked, and pressed into fiber and particle board.

In contrast to other parts of the state, which produce over 90 percent of the nation's grass seed as well as significant quantities of wheat, barley, grain, and hay, much of southwestern Oregon's economy centers around poultry, fruit, and truck farming. The land around Roseburg yields prunes, walnuts, melons, and cranberries. Dairy herds and sheep graze in the irrigated pasture lands and meadows. Around Medford, southwestern Oregon's largest city, the light fragrance of pear, peach, and apple blossoms permeates the air in spring. The sweet smells of clover and peppermint hang over Grants Pass, where in summer fields burn brilliant red, orange, and yellow with gladiola blossoms, and in early fall migrant workers move into the hop yards for the annual harvest.

Ashland has become an oasis of culture in the middle of fruit orchards and distant timber stands. The city tried to promote its mineral waters as a tourist attraction as early as 1911. That ploy failed, and Ashland waited until 1935 to try another. When a young drama professor from Southern Oregon College staged two plays by Shakespeare in the city park, promoters had so little faith in the venture that they added a boxing match to assure a profitable gate. Although the prize fight was a financial disaster, the Shakespeare Festival flourished and became one of the most acclaimed theatrical events n the nation. With each season beginning in February and running through October, the theater produces rarely performed Shakespeare plays as well as the more popular ones. A varied bill includes classical and modern plays too, such as works by Arthur Miller, Eugene O'Neill, and Tennessee Williams. During the winter, Ashland remains popular as skiers flock to the slopes of Mount Ashland, southern Oregon's premier winter sports center.

Until 1851, when two muleskinners discovered gold near Jacksonville, southwestern Oregon was largely unsettled. Stagecoaches and supply trains passed through as quickly as possible in order to avoid Indian attacks. Between 1852 and 1880, discoveries of smaller gold deposits followed at Kirby, Cave Junction, Merlin, Galice, and Canyonville. Jacksonville grew into a boom town where celebrants sometimes shot cannons in the main street, but where quick justice could be counted on. One gambler was tried, judged, hanged, and buried—all in an hour's time. Before the rush ended, over $50,000,000 in gold was taken out of Jackson, Daisy, and Applegate creeks. Enough was left for some Jacksonville residents to weather the depression of

Left: Mount Thielson's spiked summit reaches 9,182 feet as sunrise reflects on Diamond Lake, popular with fishermen and campers.

the 1930s by working the creeks and streams, and many people in the area still pan gold for fun.

The influx of miners and settlers precipitated the Rogue River Indian Wars. By 1858, when the last of the Indians had been subdued, southwestern Oregon had become a graveyard for hundreds of miners, settlers, and Indians.

The search for gold spread to other parts of southwestern Oregon — sometimes with surprising results. In 1874, Elijah Davidson followed a bear into a cave in the heart of the Siskiyou Mountains and found a labyrinth of stalactites, stalagmites, chambers and passageways. Poet, Joaquin Miller later called them the "marble halls of Oregon" and on July 9, 1909 Oregon Caves became the state's first national monument. Although there is actually only one cave, there are many rooms, most bearing names to match their formations. Outside, hiking trails into the Siskiyou Mountains offer visitors opportunities to see virgin forest and plant life ranging from giant Douglas fir and tanoak to trillium, redwood violets, and the official state flower — Oregon grape.

On the Rogue River gold was not discovered until 1859 — the year Oregon was admitted as state. Afterward, virtually every mile of the river was panned and mined. Deserted equipment, mine shafts, and diggings are still scattered along the banks.

Western novelist Zane Grey said, "The Rogue River is among the most beautiful country in the world." In the early 1920s, Grey began annual excursions to the Rogue to fish for trout, salmon, and steelhead. Later he pioneered the white-water trips that have become increasingly popular with vacationers. At least 20 companies in southern Oregon offer boat tours through the rapids.

The Rogue begins near Crater Lake and flows through five counties on its way to the Pacific Ocean. West of Grants Pass, 700-to 1,000-foot canyon walls close in on the river, and above Agness all roads cease. The river bed becomes so narrow that in places careening boats come within inches of the rocky cliffs. Ripples surge to rapids, as the whitewater churns through narrow channels. Several boaters have died at Mule Creek Canyon, where water bounces off rocks in diagonal waves, boiling eddies, and treacherous currents. At Blossom Bar, the Devil's Stairs, and the Coffee Pot, the river is a roaring roller coaster of foaming water.

For a safer, less hectic excursion into Rogue River country, many people elect to take a "mail boat" or jet boat ride from Gold Beach on the coast upriver to Galice, or to hike the 40-mile Rogue River Trail from Grave Creek to Illahe. The land along the river bank has special attraction for bird watchers and other nature lovers. Great blue heron, Roosevelt elk, and black bear may be sighted among the Oregon ash, Pacific madrone, and a profusion of wildflowers. Because much of the Rogue and its surrounding country remains undeveloped and untamed, the river was designated in 1968, as one of only eight Wild and Scenic Rivers in the nation. This act limits future development along some 80 miles of its shoreline, preserving forever this vestige of primitive America.

When a West Coast resident talks about "the Klamath," chances are he is referring to the whole region along the Oregon-California border that is drained by the rocky Klamath River. However, the Klamath Indian tribe has also lent its name to many other features in southwestern Oregon, both natural and man-made: the Klamath Mountains, which stretch from the Cascades west to the Pacific and extend their breadth southward into California; two lakes, Klamath Lake and Lower Klamath Lake (really a marsh): Fort Klamath, built during the Modoc Wars of the 1880s; Klamath County, where Indian artifacts and relics of those wars can still be found; and finally the city of Klamath Falls, which lies east of the Cascades just 25 miles from the California line.

Crater Lake, Oregon's only national park, lies in Klamath County at the southern end of the Cascades. When "Mount Mazama" began to rumble and boil 7,000 years ago, the ancestors of the Klamath Indians suspected the gods were engaged in battle and stayed away from the mountain. Soon molten lava oozed out of the sides of the mountain and weakened its foundation until the summit collapsed under its own weight. Some 17 cubic miles of lava, pumice and earth poured out at the height of the geologic violence. By the time these substances had cooled and hardened, some of the lava had traveled 35 miles, and pumice had been carried by the wind as far north as British Columbia. The caldera slowly filled with snow and rain water, which appears today as an incredible sapphire blue lake inside the volcano. At 1,932 feet, Crater Lake is the deepest lake in the United States, the second deepest in the Western Hemisphere, and the seventh deepest in the world.

*Aspen leaves and shore grasses announce an early
autumn along the shore of Upper Klamath Lake.*

The North Umpqua River runs westward from
Diamond Lake, and here at Susan Creek State Park it
flows over rock ledges where steelhead lurk in the
deep pools.

Stalactites, limestone canopies, and flowstone are the major attractions in the Oregon Caves National Monument, located southwest of Grants Pass.

Overleaf: Crater Lake fills the gigantic caldron left by the collapse of Mount Mazama about 6,500 years ago. Wizard Island was formed by later volcanic activity, but both events were witnessed by Indians.

Born near here high in the southern Cascades, the Rogue River was made famous by Zane Grey and is popular today for its fishing and white water trips.

*A V or skein of Canada geese flies over Upper
Klamath Lake on the Pacific flyway, with 9,495-foot
Mount McLoughlin in the distance.*

East of the Cascades

Over two-thirds of Oregon's 96,981 square miles lie east of the Cascade Mountains. This region is desert in that its yearly rainfall is very light. However, its terrain varies in elevation from the Wallowa Mountains in the northeast, whose Sacajawea Peak rises to 10,033 feet, to the low-lying Lava Beds in the southeast; and in surface growth from rolling ponderosa pine forests and rangelands in the center to dry desert along the Idaho border. This region symbolizes — as western Oregon does not — the traditional image of the Wild West.

In the West of the 1800s, legends were born and dreams came true. Mortals became immortal as men carved empires out of the wilderness, and fortunes were made on the turn of a shovel. The development that made this country a symbol of freedom and renewed opportunity for settlers meant death for the Indian nations and the end of freedom for a people who had hunted and roved the land for centuries. The last great Indian battles were fought on the Lava Beds. Not far away, in the late 1800s, cattle barons warred with homesteaders and sheepmen over land and water rights.

Today ghost towns weather away on lonely stretches of open land, and somewhere legendary lost gold mines wait to be found again. On the rangelands dotted with juniper and sage, petrified wood, arrowheads, and other windows to the past lie buried, awaiting discovery by collectors, archaeologists, or geologists.

The west of the nineteenth century lives on at one of the nation's oldest and most prestigious rodeos, as well as many smaller ones, and its spirit inhabits the wildlife refuges where birds and animals roam free, in the resorts and cities conceived by twentieth century empire builders, and in the cattle and sheep ranches that are still important in this country.

Chief Joseph of the Nez Perce tribe loved the 10,000-foot sunlit and snow-capped Wallowas, and he fought a hopeless battle to keep them. The "shining mountains of Oregon" were the home of the Nez Perce, and the Wallowa Valley was the "valley of the winding waters." More recently the crystal-clear lakes, white-water rivers and deep canyons in these mountains have attracted boaters and fishermen from the world over. Part of Chief Joseph's beloved lands, 220,416 acres of exposed limestone, marble ridges, and granite peaks have been set aside as the Eagle Cap Wilderness.

The Wallowas stand side-by-side with the Seven Devils Mountains of Idaho—separated by the Snake River and the deepest canyon on the North American continent. Although the Snake River is three times as long as the Hudson and forms part of the Oregon-Idaho border, it is one of our least known major waterways. When it plunges into Hells Canyon, the Snake drops 15 to 20 feet per mile. The canyon averages 5,510 feet in depth for 40 spectacular miles, and 6,000-foot depths are common. At one point, it reaches 7,900 feet—a mile and a half from river to rim, and 1,000 feet deeper than the Grand Canyon, whose maximum depth is 6,100. The sides of the canyon are so rough and steep that to reach the river can be difficult and hazardous.

But the Hells Canyon of the Snake is more than the channel of a great white-water river and the nation's deepest gorge. This part of the Snake is also one of the last strongholds for the United States' largest freshwater fish, the sturgeon, the surrounding region includes all of the life zones of North America, from the Alpine tundra of Seven Devils peaks to the desert environment at the river's edge.

In 1811, John Jacob Astor's overland party called the Snake "the accursed mad river" and left a sick man, John Day, on its banks to die. Eventually, Day recovered and, after almost a year of wandering through central Oregon, arrived in Astoria. By simply surviving, this Virginia hunter achieved immortality completely out of proportion to his accomplishments. In eastern Oregon, two rivers, a hydroelectric dam, a town, a region, and three separate sections of a national monument bear his name. The monument was not set aside to honor his memory; however, it is a priceless record in stone of how the Oregon desert country has changed through five epochs of geologic time.

The land was not always semiarid cattle country as it is today. In a day and place lost in time, the earth rumbled and cracked, releasing oceans of seething lava. The inferno of liquid stone spread like a tidal wave over the western landscape, filling valleys, choking streams, and burying and burning everything that lay before it. The seas of fire continued for perhaps centuries until all but the loftiest peaks had been covered. When the earth finally burned itself out, the largest lava plateau on the continent covered 200,000 square miles in eastern Oregon, southern Idaho and northern California. Millions of

Left: The John Day Fossil Beds National Monument has provided fossil records dating back 30 million years, including the complete evolutionary history of the horse.

years later rivers of ice chiseled and ground down the deposits, shearing off mountaintops and creating valleys, cliffs, and faults. In the period between the volcanism and the Ice Age, the landscape continued to evolve. When the climate became wet and hot, banana trees, ferns and palms blanketed eastern Oregon. Later, camels, rhinoceroses and saber-toothed tigers roamed its hills and valleys, and were joined by elephants, mammoths, and giant ground sloths.

The Owyhee, a tributary of the Snake, meanders through southeastern Oregon, between Basque settlements and sheep flocks of the Jordan Valley and Steens Mountains to the west. Like the Snake, the Owyhee is one of the most spectacular and least known rivers in the state. Petroglyphs created by ancient Indian tribes can still be seen on the sheer stone walls, and coyotes, deer, antelope, and bobcats live nearby. This is country pockmarked by ancient dry lake beds, 300-foot sand dunes, and 6,000-foot buttes. Springs come out of the rimrock, flow for a few miles, then disappear into the sand or form small alkali lakes. Greasewood and bunch grass cover miles of open country. In some places — such as the Alvord Desert, eight miles wide and 16 miles long — nothing grows. Then Steens Mountain, the world's largest block fault, rises sharply from the desert floor to an elevation of 9,670 feet.

In 1872, Peter French rode out of California and into the country west of Steens with 1,200 head of cattle. By the time an irate homesteader shot and killed him a quarter of a century later, French controlled at least 132,000 acres of southeastern Oregon. This land was eventually sold to the federal government and added to the Malheur National Wildlife Refuge, a 184,000-acre preserve for 243 species of birds and waterfowl ranging from trumpeter swans, snow geese, and sandhill cranes to tiny Audubon warblers. Bird lovers come each year to observe, study, and photograph the wildlife. Although cattle and sheep ranching are still big business, little remains to commemorate Peter French and his empire, except for the crossroads community of Frenchglen and a round barn weathering away in a field in the Blitzen Valley.

Not all of eastern Oregon's topography goes back to the Ice Age. Eleven miles south of Bend, Lava Butte rises 500 feet from the desert floor. Centuries ago molten rock spilled from the Butte's south wall, creating a lava field which spreads north and west over 6,117 acres. Twenty miles southeast of Lava Butte, East and Paulina Lakes lie inside Newberry Crater. Mount Newberry was approximately 12,000 feet high when fissures, cones and faults drained lava from its chamber and weakened the broad dome so much that it collapsed. Using carbon dating techniques, scientists have estimated that both Lava Butte and Newberry Crater are about one to two thousand years old.

Like the countryside itself, Bend, Sun River, and Kah-Nee-Ta Resort are relatively recent developments. While Bend's primary industries are lumber and wood products, it is also the hub for recreational activities that range from skiing at Mount Bachelor to superb fishing, boating, and swimming in numerous lakes and rivers. Lava Butte is a favorite haunt of rockhounds, and hikers find new challenges among the spectacular monoliths in Smith Rock State Park.

Today, the spirit of the empire builders manifests itself in planned communities and resort complexes. Sun River, which one magazine called "the healthiest town in America," is the dream and development of principally one man — Portland industrialist, John Gray. It has 14 tennis courts, 18 miles of bicycle paths, a golf course, riding stables, and the Deschutes River for fishing. During the summer, an average of 300 airplanes per week — many of which are private jets — fly into its airport.

Kah-Nee-Ta Resort, which features an ultra modern arrowhead shaped lodge, a golf course, and Indian teepees that vacationers can rent by the day or week, is owned and managed by the Confederated Tribes of the Warm Springs Indians. The reservation and confederation are equivalent to an individual national government.

Each September since 1910, the traditional Wild West of bucking horses, cattle roping, and bull dogging has been revived for one week at the Pendleton Round-Up. The community has become so firmly associated with rodeos, woolen shirts, and blankets, that few realize that Pendleton's economy is really rooted in its spacious wheat fields, its rows of peas, and bush beans, and its timber, or that the largest manufacturer of unfinished furniture in the world is headquartered here.

Any portrait of Oregon must of necessity be filled with multiple images. Each part of this state is rich in history and possesses a wealth of natural beauty.

Golden wildflowers line the crevices of the Painted Hills, adding a delicate counterpoint to its barren surface.

Overleaf: Bands of mineral deposits inspired the name Painted Hills for this section of the John Day Fossil Beds in Wheeler County.

73

An old barn remains structurally sound in the
dry air of the semiarid eastern Oregon steppe not far
from Mitchell.

Meadows and pine forests surround the cool,
blue waters of Anthony Lakes while beyond, in the
Elkhorn Range of the Blue Mountains, a ski and
sports area operates during the winter.

Its broad valley is a springtime patchwork of farms as the Grande Ronde River wanders past La Grande, Elgin, and Troy before joining the Snake River.

*The Crooked River winds close to the base of
pinnacles and spires rising abruptly from lava plains
at Smith Rock State Park north of Bend.*

Wildflowers on Summit Prairie form a carpet beneath tall ponderosa pines in the Ochoco Range.